DIAMOND BO

GW00727931

The Creation Series
BOOK 1
God's World

Written by Carole Leah
Illustrated by Sharon Lewis

1

Dear Parents and Teachers

Diamond Books is a collection of books based on the Bible to help 3-9 year olds develop their reading skills.

This book is the first in a series of eight based on the 'Genesis' account in the Good News Bible. It has been written from a Judeo-Christian viewpoint. It is intended to be read <u>to</u> 3-4 year olds. The whole series prepares children to read and extend their vocabulary. In this book (in conjunction with other materials - see page 27 for details) children can develop and practise preparatory skills for reading.

Encourage children to :-

- <u>FIND</u> THE PICTORIAL SNAILS AND COUNT THEM.
- <u>LEARN</u> THE BIBLE VERSE AND ITS REFERENCE (see page 24).
- <u>SEQUENCE</u> THE NUMBER OF DAYS IN A WEEK.
- <u>TALK</u> ABOUT THE ILLUSTRATIONS.
- <u>SORT</u> DIFFERENT ITEMS OF CREATION ACCORDING TO SIZE, SHAPE AND COLOUR.

Biblical quotations are in bold type throughout and some biblical concepts, shown by asterisks, are explained on page 25. Some words may need explaining to the children. These are listed on the same page. Further activities for the emergent reader are suggested in the accompanying workbook (see page 27).

'God's World' emphasises the wonder of God's order in creation.

Meet Todd, Joy and Daniel

See what they are doing in this book!

Joy is just 4.

Todd is 4 and nearly 5.
Todd comes to stay
with Joy and Daniel often.

Daniel is only 3.
Joy and Daniel are brother
and sister.

Look for the snails!

How many snails can you find in this book?

(Answer is on page 26)

Did you know that snails have no legs?

3

In the beginning

God made the heavens and

the Earth.

God spoke and

everything was made in

just a few days.*

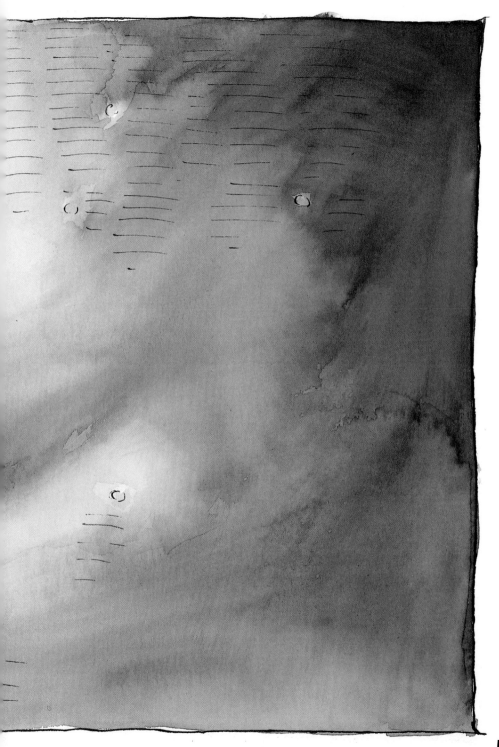

5

Day one

God made bright light.

Evening passed and

morning came -

that was the first day.

Day two

God made the big sky.

Evening passed and

morning came -

that was the second day.

Day three

God made the huge sea.

He made the dry land.

He made all kinds of plants.

Evening passed and

morning came -

that was the third day.

Day four

God made all the shining lights above

the sky.

Evening passed and

morning came -

that was the fourth day.

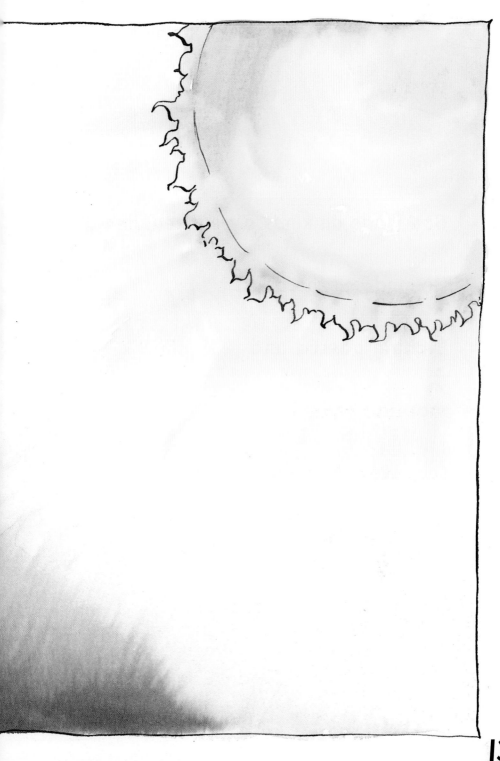

Day five

God made all kinds of sea creatures.

He made all the birds.

Evening passed and

morning came -

that was the fifth day.

14

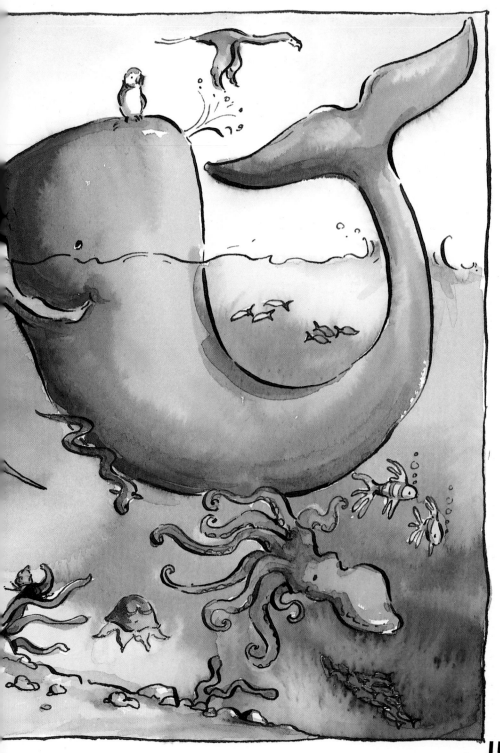

Day six

God made all kinds of land animals and

the first people.

Evening passed and

morning came -

that was the sixth day.

God made all these things in

just six days.

God looked at everything he had made.

He was very pleased.

Everything was so good!

Day seven

God finished making his world.

He rested.

God **blessed the seventh day.**

God made it a special day.

Now, Todd, Joy and Daniel are happy because everything belongs to God.

God is their Father.

God is our Father, too!

God, **you made the world and**

everything in it.

Psalm 89, verse 11

WORDS TO EXPLAIN TO YOUNG CHILDREN

Ensure that the children know the meaning of all these words:-

blessed   - set apart, made happy, made beautiful, wished well

heavens - the sky as seen from the Earth, in which the sun, moon and stars appear

huge   - very, very, very, very big

special - different, very loved

spoke   - said with a voice, talked

OOTNOTES FOR ADULTS (asterisked from main text)

The Bible clearly states that God created the universe in six literal days. Ken Ham in his book 'The Lie-Evolution' (published by 'Answers in Genesis', PO Box 5262, LEICESTER, LE2 3XU) states:-
"The word for 'day' in Genesis 1 is the Hebrew word 'yom'. It can mean either a day (in the ordinary 24-hour day), the daylight portion of an ordinary 24-hour day (i.e. the day as distinct from the night), or occasionally it is used in the sense of an indefinite period of time (e.g., 'In the time of the Judges' or 'In the day of the Lord'). Without exception, in the Hebrew Old Testament the word 'yom' never means 'period' (i.e. it is never used to refer to a definite long period of time with specific beginning and end points). The word which means a long period of time in Hebrew is 'olam'. Furthermore, it is important to note that even when the word 'yom' is used in the indefinite sense, it is clearly indicated by the context that the literal meaning of the word 'day' is not intended.
Some people say the word 'day' in Genesis may have been used symbolically and is thus not meant to be taken literally. However, an important point that many fail to consider is that a word can never be symbolic for the first time it is used! In fact a word can only be used symbolically when it has first had a literal meaning."
Other parts of the Bible confirm the six literal days of creation eg: Exodus 20:11 and Exodus 31:17. 2 Peter 3:1-7 refers to the time of creation, not an evolving beginning. The details of creation are repeated in other parts of the Bible eg: 2 Kings 19:15; 1 Chronicles 16:26; Psalm 33:6-9; Psalm 74:16 Psalm 102:25; Psalm 104:19; Isaiah 40:28; Isaiah 66:2; Mark 10:5-6; Acts 17:26; Hebrews 1:10; and Revelation 10:6.

REFERENCES

Biblical References

p6	Genesis 1:5
p8	Genesis 1:8
p10	Genesis 1:13
p12	Genesis 1:19
p14	Genesis 1:23
p16	Genesis 1:31
p18	Genesis 1:31
p20	Genesis 2:3

'Snail' References

11 in total:-

on pages 3 (3), 15, 17, 18, 19, 20 and 22
(and on front and back covers!)

OTHER MATERIALS IN PREPARATION:-

In order for young children to develop the skills for reading they need to follow through desirable learning outcomes. The following additional materials help with these:-

A **Photocopiable Workbook** (including worksheets) to help a child's personal and social development, language and literacy, mathematics, knowledge and understanding of the world, physical development (hand-eye co-ordination) and creative development

An enjoyable **Audio Cassette** to help with aural discrimination

An **Audio Music Cassette** and **Songbook**

A **Set of Large Posters** incorporated into a **Big Flipbook**

ALSO IN PREPARATION:-

SETS 'B' AND 'C' FOR 4-5 YEAR OLDS
(In keeping with the National Literacy Strategy
Vocabulary Lists for Reception)

8 pre-readers and **8 main readers** of **The 'Jesus' Series**
(Set B)

8 readers of **The 'God and Me' Series** (Set C)

Photocopiable Workbooks

Simple Dictionaries

Audio Cassettes to help learn the alphabet and develop
listening skills

Alphabet Chart

Audio Music Cassettes and **Songbooks**

Large Posters incorporated into **Big Flipbooks**